A second Copy
for Sister Teresa -
Carmel at
Saranac Lake .

with my love
and blessing!
Alfred Barrett, S.J.

August 18 1954.

Don't lose it!

MINT BY NIGHT

MINT
BY
NIGHT

ALFRED BARRETT, S.J.

THE AMERICA PRESS

NEW YORK CITY

To

MY MOTHER

ACKNOWLEDGMENTS

For permission to reprint certain of the poems in this book, the author wishes to thank the editors of *America, The Ave Maria, Columbia, The Commonweal, The Far East, Jesuit Missions, The Queen's Work* and *Spirit*.

CONTENTS

I

II

III

IV

I

Mint by Night

So quickly to have lost the summertime
Sends me home heartsick. Up the bank I climb
Trampling the hidden mint. I pause, and then
One breath of mint evokes all summer again.

You groping poets, blinded by too much
Of sea and sky, of taste and smell and touch,
Come out some night of tears and feel with me
How subtly mint assuages misery.

For mint by day is little more than grass
Tempting the casual cattle as they pass;
But mint by night is like the Holy Ghost,
Making its nearness known when needed most.

All redolent with promises of bright
Eternal summers to come is mint by night.
Come out and tramp with me some field untrod
When mint is like the very breath of God.

Summer must go and darkness come and death,
But night is heavy with God's very breath.
I will remember mint when frost comes on
And boughs are leafless and the last bird gone.

Two Carthaginian Girls

Walking at night-fall where the pink
And red hibiscus trimly furls,
I watch two petals blow to the grass,
Two crimson stains to make me think
Upon those Carthaginian girls,
Perpetua, Felicitas,
Whose very names our missals link
In perpetual felicity.

Blurred centuries dissolve. I see
A martyr walking to her crown,
Pale as her ungirded gown,
The tall, serene, patrician
Perpetua . . . . Felicitas,
Of humbler origin, a slave,
Nurses her dungeon-born with tears,
Her babe of two brief days. Some man
Derides her travail pain and sneers,
"How against beasts will you be brave?"
To whom the martyr makes reply,
"I suffer now, but when I die
Christ suffers in me then, not I."
They wait unseeing side by side,
When over the arena sands
Races a tawny, snarling tide,
A surf of lions circling round,
Lions that cringe and paw the ground—
For suddenly no spear can prod
Them on to where Perpetua stands
Like a light-house shining out to God
With the white beams of extended hands.

[4]

Careless of death, its when and how,
Perpetua, Felicitas,
The mistress and the serving lass,
Encircle one another's necks,
Embracing, till a goaded cow
Is loosed to match and mock their sex.
Perpetua is tossed. She falls
Piteously. The heifer mauls
With violating horns. But she
Arises, mangled, smoothes her dress
And drapes that riven tunic, less
Mindful of pain than modesty.
Then gathering her streaming hair
In the pathos of her womanly pride,
Begs for some clasp. With skill and care
Both arms sweep in fluent curves
To her head, that, though her robes be torn,
His eyes whom she dying serves
May deem her vain as any bride
And not as one who seems to mourn . . . .
Two Carthaginian girls, they kneel,
Perpetua, Felicitas,
Upon their lifted throats to feel
The sacrificial *coup-de-grâce*,
The stroke of consecrating steel.

So far away and long ago
These girls were born and loved and died,
It daily sets my heart aglow
To see—like petals side by side—
Perpetua, Felicitas
Pressed in the Canon of the Mass!

[5]

The Rosebush and the Trinity

Saint John Damascene
Thought a man might see
The semblance of the Trinity,
The how and why of One and Three
(Father, Son and Holy Ghost)
In a rosebush most.

Tonight I mean to walk
From book
To bower—
Intently look
At the paternal stalk
Lifting the filial flower—
Be aware
Of both of them,
Bloom and stem,
Before I see the bush or yet draw near it—
The rose's triune beauty finally share,
Led by its essence loosed upon the air,
As on our world is breathed the Holy Spirit!

I thank John Damascene
For pages that disclose
To me
(If not the Trinity)
More about the rose.

Saint Bernard

Being a poet
  I had rather
Written as Bernard
  Of God the Father
Son and Holy Ghost
  Than penned the pleas
Of passion Abelard
  Sent Heloïse.
Bernard is writing,
  The monks said when the snow
Drove like a quill
  Through the cloisters of Clairvaux.
Bernard is praying,
  And a smile of stone
On the Virgin's statue melts
  To flesh and bone.
Bernard is dying,
  A poet's angel said.
Jesu, Jesu dulcis . . .
  Bernard is dead.
Here's my hosanna
  To Bernard the bard
Who wrote love letters
  Better than Abelard!

Saint Thomas More to Margaret

How now, daughter Margaret?
    What now, Mother Eve?
Lurks some serpent in thy breast
    Musing to deceive,
To proffer Father Adam
    The apple once again?
Nay, I have shaped my conscience,
    Though I judge not other men,
And thee, mine own sweet Meg, I love
    Too much that to thy shame
I should forswear God's favor
    To win the King's acclaim.
If but I die right merrily,
    Though I feel me faint,
Die as the Baptist, Cyprian
    And many a hapless saint,
God will not leave me to be lost.
    Think how upon His knee—
As once thyself thy father, Meg—
    He dandleth me!

Cyrano of the Saints

Prince Aloysius, who is she whose eyes
Force you to kneel before her and to rise
Bondsman to maiden's beauty? Who is she
For whom you keep such stately courtesy?
Do you recall now, threadbare courtier,
The days you fought for happiness and her?
Do you recall how anxiously she prayed
As the swift anger of your rapier blade
Harried a hundred foemen? She awoke
Strange fire in your soul, strengthened your stroke,
Made Heaven's veteran of earth's recruit.
The night your snowy plume in proud salute
Swept the blue threshold of your Lady's door
It had not ever touched the ground before!

Repartee

Because her bucking cart-mule
  Showed scant respect for a saint,
There rose from a ditch near *Medina*
  Del Campo this complaint:

"Why do You treat me thus, dear Lord?
  I'd willingly shed my blood,
But I balk at the prospect of martyrdom
  In this Castilian mud."

Smiled Christ—"Thus do I treat My friends,
  So must I thus treat you."
"No wonder, Lord," sighed Teresa,
  "No wonder You have so few!"

Saint Francis de Sales

The cold syllogism
    To confute avails,
Yet leaves the heart in schism—
    Muses de Sales.

With God's warmth of grace in me
    I may yet convince
The heart, as at Annecy
    Yellows the quince.

Auriesville Birches

I

Who has but eyes to see and hands to feel
Must know that these
Thickets of thinning trees,
Beneath which children romp, were not all scarred
By linked initials of long-vanished lovers.
Holier names—who knows?—this ringed growth
    covers,
Carved by a Blackrobe's courtly fingers, hard
With the tussling of a hundred portage marches;
Whose fashion it was to steal—
Dreaming of Gothic naves, rose-windows and pointed
    arches—
Into this grove, at dawn his boughy church,
Who, lacking reliquary,
Deep in the pliant silver of this birch
Sealed the soft name: Mary.

II

Lonely missionaries mark
    Jesus on the birches, *Mary,*
Joseph, and the silver bark
    Is a silver reliquary.

What will strangers think who trace,
    Some far June, this carving? Only
That this was a trysting place,
    That some lover once was lonely.

Mother Seton at Emmitsburg

Hers was a country where the axes rang
To hew a vista letting in the sun;
The logs had hardly fallen when they sprang
Foursquare and fragrant—and the house was done.
Something is lost that she knew when our land
Had to be cleared and set with barriers,
For wheat-fields wave only when fences stand,
And water only flows from springs like hers.

Thickets of tangled thought are on us now,
The springs are choked and all the fences down.
She must have known, and planned with placid brow
Outposts in many a countryside and town,
Where nuns in softer days might still pioneer—
Facing in each young mind a new frontier.

Saint Therese of Lisieux

Not as a prima donna in a pose
Before the swaying curtain when the play
Is clamorously ended, her bouquet
Loosed on the throng,—not even as a rose
Can I conceive of you. Let others, those
Whose lyric season is incessant May,
Cull similes to strew your "little way"
With hothouse verse and honeysuckle prose.

You are too real, too actual, Therese,
To live in metaphor. The girl behind
The legend, could the legend fade, would be
The girl you were, sobbing upon your knees
In lowliness and love and anguish, blind
With the beauty of a stark Gethsemane.

A Martyr's Mass

*Father Miguel Pro, S.J., executed at Mexico
City, November 23, 1927*

Kneeling he spoke the Names he loved the most
    As the air was fanned by the whir of invisible wings;
He seemed like a priest about to breathe on the Host
    After the *Sanctus* rings.

"This is My Body," he said on his First-Mass Day,
    When the rose of priesthood slipped its snowy bud.
Lifting his chaliced heart now could he say
    At death, "This is My Blood."

Swift as an altar chime the rifles rang . . .
    The stole of crimson flowing over his breast,
How bright it burned, and how his sealed lips sang
    The *Ite, Missa Est!*

II

The Singers of Della Robbia

Three Florentines in stone, three singing boys
Inhabit all my dreams, their heads apoise,
Lips shaped to a song that never leaves their throats.
Pity the sculptor, dying, with the notes
Of their *Adeste* yet unheard! Who are
These voiceless singers? Angels?—when the star
Like a rose-window shines and plain-chant swells
From the rounded mouths of a million Gabriels?
The youngest angels at the Crib, who saw
Beauty Incarnate lying in the straw
And fell to dreaming and forgot to sing?
Through Gothic centuries the minsters ring
With antiphons of Bethlehem. Alone
Three singing boys, three Florentines in stone,
Spreading a sculptured scroll, wait breathlessly
Like angel altos listening for their key!

Brevity

Blessed be Luke who gives the signs
And lets me read between the lines!

With the manger in my mind I'm able
To rear an angel-raftered stable.

Seeing the swaddling clothes I know
God it was that dwindled so.

Saint Luke knew poets would supply
Mary's Chaldean lullaby.

Franciscan Church, New York

The green star of a traffic light, aglow
Like the Magi's reappearing guide, says *Go!*
Enter the house and find the holy Child,
The house is near, how very near you know.

None seem to know—in earshot of the L,
Hard by a huge Herodian hotel,
While taxis quarrel in the canyon streets—
That in their midst is born Emmanuel.

None but a few who turn with me to feel
The wood beneath, about us as we kneel—
An oaken altar and a crib of pine,
Rafters of wood instead of stone and steel.

Chromium is ore that never lived, but wood
Boasts in its birthday grain of years it stood
Lithe on a firry headland. Chosen once
For cradle and for cross, God found it good.

Brown as a friar's cowl with candle-smoke,
This is His house of whom Saint Francis spoke,
And whom Saint Francis honored in His birth,
Hewing the first crib from the living oak.

Yet, near the breadline where the poor are fed
By poor Assisians with more than bread,
Men tongue hosannas to the gods of greed,
Oblivious of all Saint Francis said.

Rivers of human souls that swerve and pour
Through water-wheels of that department store,

If they have heard good tidings of great joy,
Here are the gifts they should be shopping for.

Three trickling streams that day-long never cease
Know this church as a delta of release
From silt of sin. Three tributaries flow
Through these three doors into the gulf of peace.

The rest are whelmed in clamor where the tall
And shining shafts proclaim that size is all;
While God—immense—who dwindled to a Babe
Sleeps in the midst of it as in a stall.

Stille Nacht

Ah, yesterday was Christmas in Berlin!
    The papers did not print it, but I saw
Storm troopers turn Saint Joseph from the inn,
    And beds for only cattle in the straw.

Two thousand years, Lord, and we had not heard
    (Nicea spoke of God becoming man)
How in the stillness of the night Thy Word
    Leapt down from Heaven, being made Aryan!

Yet children journeyed—in their dreams—beyond
    Berlin to Bethlehem, and there they knew
The Babe of Mary was not really blond,
    When to their German hearts they clasped a Jew.

The Silent Saint

Plumed with shavings like a swan,
  The plane of a Carpenter glides and sings.
Gold shavings rustle on the floor,
  One to a Child's gold ringlet clings.

On the gravel whispers a trailing gown,
  Whisper the leaves on the garden walk.
Hushed is noon to a Maid's shy footstep—
  Why should Joseph want to talk?

Talitha Cumi

Talitha cumi!
  Maiden, arise!
Maiden, maiden,
  Open your eyes!
Daughter of Jairus,
  Rise from the dead;
Jesus is bending
  Over your bed.
Soon at the cistern
  Village girls
Will shoulder their pitchers
  And tossing their curls
Will turn at your coming
  And widen their eyes.
Talitha cumi,
  Maiden, arise!
Bending, bending
  Over your head,
Talitha cumi,
  Jesus said,
Framed by the fringe
  Of your opening eyes—
Talitha cumi,
  Damsel, arise!

The Undiminished Bread

He multiplied five loaves of wheat
    To feed the multitude,
Dreaming of when mankind might eat
    More than ephemeral food.
"Unless the planted grain be dead
It bringeth forth no fruit," He said.

Thus for our hunger's surfeiting
    The Grain of God was sown,
To die, be buried, and to spring
    Bright from the bursting stone—
The Wheat, the undiminished Bread
Of multitudes unborn, unfed.

Chant of Departure

A missionary's prayer

Woman who walked home on the arm of John
Another way from that your Son had gone,
Woman who walked
And talked,
Unwavering, of what must yet be done—
Woman, behold your son!

Behold
Him who in boyhood haunts will not grow old;
Who goes predestined to an alien grave
In clay or sand or wave—
Yet sails enamored of one hope: to see,
As John from his dawn-lit boat on Galilee,
Christ in the haze-dim faces on the shore
At Shantung or the coast of Travancore.

Woman who walked home on the arm of John,
When on
Some night of tears I hear the palm trees toss,
Stand by my side beneath the Southern Cross.

Mary's Assumption

Factum est silentium in coelo, quasi media hora
                    Apocalypse: viii, 1

There was silence in heaven, as if for half an hour—
    Isaian coals of wonder sealed the lips
Of seraph, principality and power,
    Of all the nine angelic fellowships.

The archangels, those sheer intelligences,
    Were silent, with their eyes on heaven's door.
(So must our fancy dower them with senses,
    Make them incarnate in a metaphor.)

There was silence in heaven as Mary entered in,
    For even Gabriel had not foreseen
The glory of a soul immune from sin
    Throned in the body of the angels' Queen.

Blessed be God and Mary in whose womb
    Was woven God's incredible disguise!
She gave Our Lord His Body. In the tomb
    He gave her hers again and bade her rise.

Bright from death's slumber she arose, the flush
    Of a chaste joy illumining her cheeks.
Among the motherless in heaven there was a hush
    To hear the way a mother laughs and speaks.

Eye had not seen, nor ear of angel heard,
    Nor heart conceived—until Our Lady's death—

What God for those that love Him had prepared
    When heaven's synonym was Nazareth!

Her beauty opened slowly, like a flower,
    Beauty to them eternally bequeathed.
There was silence in heaven, as if for half an hour
    No angel breathed.

III

Wedded

There's a linnet that warbles at evening, that warbles,
A last linnet that warbles—
   He is warbling now!

Wind-whispers are stirring, subsiding and stirring,
Wind-whispers are stirring
   The bloom-laden bough.

Steps sound on the gravel, feet crunch the blue gravel,
Steps sound on the gravel,
   There's a rush to the door.

A shower of kisses, of laughter and kisses,
A shower of kisses,
   And "More, daddy, more!"

The clinking of silver, of glassware and silver,
The clinking of silver,
   The chiming of clocks;

Then the exquisite tinkle, the quavering tinkle,
The honey-toned tinkle
   Of a Swiss music-box.

Two alone with the roses their garden encloses,
Two alone with the roses
   At the dusk of day;

And only the fireflies, the acolyte fireflies,
The green-twinkling fireflies
   Hear what they say.

Mon Repos

My mother's girlhood home

The orange-tree you planted as a bride
At Mon Repos, long years ago has died;
And now the weeping willow, trailing low
Over the drive, is gone from Mon Repos.

There was a welcome in that willow's boughs,
Their sweep announced the hostess and the house:
The coachman and his pair no longer know
The feel of willow, entering Mon Repos.

Old friends who came there of a holiday
Were eager for the hostess' "Won't you stay?"—
Discourteous Death to some has whispered "Go!",
And they have gone, and so has Mon Repos.

And all the loveliness we called our own
Has gone. Wistaria's fountain spray wind-blown,
Showering rose-fringed lawns with summer snow,
Has felt the touch of frost with Mon Repos.

The orange-tree you planted never grew.
Wistaria and willow pass. But you,
More dear than memories of long ago,
Are all I care to keep of Mon Repos.

Her Sewing Room

Why do I pause and listen
  As one who faintly hears
The humming of her whirling wheel,
  The snipping of her shears?
There's never a winding stair I climb
  But makes me think again
I hear these things, and all my soul
  Is listening, and then . . .
Spun on the loom of quiet song
  In the throat where mirth is made,
The severed thread of her silken laugh
  Drifts over the balustrade.
All day her cuckoo-clock keeps ticking
  Summoning me still
Her skeins of yarn to tangle,
  Her button trays to spill.
And sometimes with a jealous pang
  I'm wondering why she,
Alone with her spools and needlework,
  Is never seen by me;
But seen by the chirping cuckoo
  When the hour strikes with a whir,
Weaving garments of simple cloth
  For children woven of her.

Her Looking-glass

No mercurial calendar
Truly tells how old you are,
Lacking the poet's truer tongue
Who looks at you and calls you young;
Young, though the years have combed away
Hair that was glossy once to gray.
The childless women, the selfish wives,
I pity their strange and lonely lives
(While reverencing the childing pain
Of those who have nursed a dream in vain);
And I hold that beauty early fails
The woman who thinks that lacquered nails
And the silk she puts upon her back
Avail to cheat the almanac.
The childless woman, her glass to her
Is a harsh and dubious flatterer.
But the years will gently deal as they pass
With you, who have had for looking-glass—
Unflanked by vials of scented waters—
The admiring eyes of admired daughters.

Unearth

Her daughter takes the veil

Gardener of Eden and Gethsemane,
Gently unearth this rosebush that has grown
In the sunken garden of my heart, and be
Gentle to her who yields it yet unblown.
Gardener of Eden, where this tender stem
Henceforth will know the strength of other fingers,
And these leaves brush another's garment hem—
You will not care if round the root there lingers
Something of native soil to swell the bud
Till that root sinks in You as once in me . . .
Unearth the rosebush of my flesh and blood,
Gardener of Eden—and Gethsemane!

IV

Hands of a Priest

I gaze in quiet wonder at each hand
As one who knows yet strives to understand
Their new-found range.
Strange
That I feel no change
Who lately felt the firm anointing thumb
That sealed these palms with power, heard the *Come,
Holy Ghost!* intoned, and watched the linen band
Bind each to each.
Long had I feared that this my fingers clasp
Lay far beyond my grasp.
What is there now that lies beyond my reach?

Hands of a priest, my hands, you still will clutch
At evil, but to whiten not to smutch
The souls that feel your more-than-Midas touch.

Hands of a priest, my hands, the God you serve
Because He shaped you, flesh and bone and nerve,
Will nestle in the cradle of your curve.

My Yoke is sweet and Oh! my Burden light.
As I walk forth tonight,
He on Whose breast I may not yet recline
Leans on mine!

Linen

Lo, how the acolyte
  Tiptoes, lest wax
Drip on the altar-cloth's
  Consecrate flax,
The linen, the linen
  Where lately has lain
Whiteness on whiteness
  And will lie again . . .

See how in God's design,
  Layette to mound,
A lifetime of linen
  Laps us round.
In homes and in sacristies
  Heaped on shelves
Is whiteness integral
  With ourselves.
For swaddling the newly-born
  Linen is pure,
For coif, amice,
  Sepulture.
Linen is holy
  That cradles the head
Of a mother who swathes,
  In her smooth marriage-bed,
Her infant in linen
  And holds him high
To live in linen
  Until he die—

And, dying in linen
  From shoulders to feet,
To rise like Lazarus
  In a winding-sheet.

The Vows of Religion

"Waste not thy substance," Wisdom saith.
  Have I been wise in prodigally giving,
  While living,
What might be hoarded in my heart till death?

The will, the elemental drive
  To quarry and plan deliberately and rear
  And dwell therein was dear
To me as it is to any man alive.

This is my very substance, yes,
  This which I freely, prodigally gave
  Is what the grave
Would someday grimly take, no more, no less.

Death men obey, made poor, made coldly chaste—
  Death I will cheat,
  Living to loose this chrism on Christ's feet.
Wisdom will never ask me, "Why this waste?"

There Must Be Tears

And God shall wipe away all tears from their eyes
Apocalypse: vii, 17

The fog of why men suffer only clears
When Revelation lances down its ray:
If Heaven will be the banishing of tears,
There must be tears for God to wipe away.

The Candle

Slender and firm,
  Whatever be its height,
Changing its body
  Into heat and light,
The candle seems growing
  From the candlestick,
As if an unblown yellow rose
  Bloomed on the wick.
Lord, like this candle
  Am I, who aspire
To consume my body
  In my spirit's fire,
Who from my mother's womb,
  As beeswax from the hive,
Was shaped by Thy molding
  To be with light alive.
Lord, in this candle
  Here I stand.
Lift me from the candlestick,
  Hold me in Thy hand!

Discipline

Beauty with metric discipline
Hems in
The stanzas written by the stars,
The rings of Saturn and the moons of Mars.
Even these rhymes,
Balanced along the taut
And tenuous tight-rope of a thought,
Should the slow-pacing rhythm falter,
Slip into prose.
Think how the trellised rose,
Most dutiful
Obsequious votary at Beauty's altar,
Unhampered climbs,
More beautiful
For having known restraint;
And how the saint,
Beauty's ordained precision to fulfill,
Moves in the orbit of God's holy will.

Incense

Incense is prayer
  That drives no bargain.
Child, learn from incense
  How best to pray.
Incense—abused
  In rhymesters' jargon—
Curls through my stanzas,
  Pungent, gray,
That eye and nostril,
  Scent and sight
May thrill with the mounting
  Clouds of spice,
Rising like prayer
  For God's delight,
Whenever a thurible
  Swings high thrice.

Incense is praise
  Past all devising
Beautiful, natural,
  Perfect praise.
Child, from your soul
  Incense is rising
As from a thurible.
  Spend your days
Thus, ashamed to be
  Questing pelf,
To nag at God
  With importunate palm,

When incense, like goodness,
   Diffuses itself—
Rising like the *Gloria*
   At the end of a psalm!

Conjecture

"Poilu of France!" a voice cries, sabres gleam
Around the Eternal Flame, that tombstone of fire
Where lies an unknown soldier who did not desire
His anonymous grave, whose dying dream
Was a wooden cross with his name. On German sod
His enemy sleeps in the Ehrenmal, unknown.
Who are these men? Conjecture pries the stone
Where each waits to be identified by God.

Maybe one groans, beneath the Eternal Flame
To alien dirges horribly awake:
"I am Franz Bischof, *Ober-leutnant,*
10th Wurtembergers!" Maybe one says: "My name
Is Simonson," as he hears the Horst Wessel chant,
"I am a Jew! There must be some mistake."

Ferdinand Foch

A man in horizon-blue, whose breast is free
From the bars and ribbons his lieutenants wear,
At the rosary's ending kisses reverently
His only *Croix-de-guerre*.

Pius XI: Mountaineer

He took the crozier for the alpenstock
Of Monte Rosa and the Brenner Pass,
Henceforth a lowland shepherd where the grass
Grew lush for his illimitable flock.
Danger had nerved him young to sense the shock
And earth-tilt of the avalanche. Alas!
Still for the witless yawns the fresh crevasse:
The wise are they who stand on solid rock.

The world is snowed in on a mountain-slope—
Rescue is in the Voice that none will hear,
Expounding his technique of axe and rope
To scale secure the last long kilometer.
O world be wise and heed Christ's Mountaineer
And hear your boots ring on the Rock of Peter!

Bookplate for Saint Ambrose

Non in dialectica complacuit Deo salvum facere
populum suum
— Saint Ambrose

Turn but the parchment of this crackling tome
For food on which both head and heart may feed,
Sweetly persuasive, like the honeycomb
Christ ate to prove that He was risen indeed.

The Novice

*Your old men shall dream dreams, and your young
men shall see visions*
                                          Joel: ii, 28

The timid stars their faces faintly show
Like blue-veiled nuns but lately come from prayer.
Beyond the cloister sombre cedars wear
Monastic habits of wind-mounded snow,
Dreaming old dreams no novice yet may know;
While twilight, sacristan serenely fair,
Quenches the candles distantly aflare
Upon the altar of the afterglow.

Visions, not dreams, for me who am not old!
(Visions are lent to youth and dreams deferred
Until the rosary of tears is told)
Visions like mine tonight: day dim with rose,
As here I watch my *Ave,* like a bird,
Go singing down the path the sunset goes!

Instinct

When God unfolds the blueprints
    In a bluebird's brain,
Somehow it scans the self-same plans
    And builds a nest again.

The Siege of the Alcazar

Toledo, as El Greco saw it, misty and blue and still,
The minarets of the City of God, alhambras on a hill—
July, and the chrism of sunlight anoints the queenly
    town,
Wearing the river like a train, the castle like a crown,
The castle of the Alcazar, the fort where Spanish youth
Conspires with beauty to defend the citadel of truth.

But beauty's hands are bound
When the guns begin to pound.

The hammer-and-sickle waves in Spain and Falsehood
    swings a scythe
More deadly than the arcs of lead that sweep where
    victims writhe,
Honed on the wheel of Moscow—yet destined here
    to shiver
Against a rock that crowns a town whose train is a
    trailing river.

Girls in the plaza dance. (Cadets
Dance to machine-gun castanets!)

Death is a better Spain to men who see God banned
    from Spain.
On the foreheads of babies, dungeon-born, each swears
    till none remain
To hold this fortress of the faith or perish at his post
As an avenger of that sin against the Holy Ghost.

Christ's matadors, they bait the bull
With blood in a gesture beautiful.

Though bombs rain and mines blast, hell cannot hope
    to humble
Men who have seen the roof-trees of convents flare and
    crumble,
Who exorcise with the sacred sign the whine that comes
    from hell,
Like the shout of a fallen angel, of each blaspheming
    shell.

Ten weeks the steel took wing, until
One day the storming guns were still.

The admired miracle is known, the enemy inventory
Of caissons emptied; but the world has censored from
    the story
The might of Our Lady of Montserrat and her surpass-
    ing aid,
Before whose shrine *hidalgos* sheathe and pledge a vo-
    tive blade.
For dread that where Loyola knelt no sword might
    hang again,
Isaian anger lit their souls, Moscardó and his men.

It seemed to them Ignatius yet
Rose on Pamplona's parapet,
Sharing Toledo's blood and sweat;
As if Teresa too had come
(Once "for the Moors and martyrdom")
To win her martyr's palm at home—
Through daughters, fled from Spain to God,
Cloistered by the firing-squad!

The Wolverine

At evening when Poughkeepsie's bridge
Shrinks into shadow, when the ridge
Across the Hudson sharper grows,
Each pine top stencilled on gold and rose,
Out from the granite cliff I lean
To watch the hurtling *Wolverine*
Thunder past with a snort and a scream
And a flare of flame in its plume of steam.
Its windows fuse in a sweep of light
That curves like a scimitar through the night;
And keen as a sword there comes to me
A poignant rush of sympathy
For all the passion and all the pain
That flashes by with the roar of the train.
The train is gone. Serene and slow
Home on the hem of night I go.
The hills resume their broken dream
And silence surges out on the stream.

Boat Song of the Voyageur

How blue the stream with our Queen's own blue
  And the isles we pass how green!
And our hearts how warm with the love of you,
  Isle named for our blue-gowned Queen!
Then home on the stream of a thousand isles
  To the isle we long to see,
Till over the watery way for miles
    Chime the bells of Sault Sainte Marie,
              Marie!
    The bells of Sault Sainte Marie!

Carillons sing of our blue-gowned Queen,
  But none like the wild cascades!
Oh, none like the organ-toned Lachine,
  Nor the dipping paddle blades!
So home on the stream of a thousand isles
  To the isle we long to see,
Till over the watery way for miles
    Chime the bells of Sault Sainte Marie,
              Marie!
    The bells of Sault Sainte Marie!

Bird of God

*To the memory of Father Philip Delon, S.J., and
Father William F. Walsh, killed in the crash
of the mission plane Marquette*

There came a sound from heaven as of a wind
Mighty and sudden . . . So the Paraclete
Descended on mankind,
Descended till the Fishermen could feel the hovering
  pinions beat.
There came a sound from heaven, answering,
With whistle of straining wing,
Alaska's *Come, Holy Ghost!* The air was stirred
By the thunderous, whirlwind passage of a Bird.

God made all flying things,
Eagle and albatross,
With tapered body and spread of outstretched wings
To hang against the sunset like a cross.
Thus, on a cross, before the breathless dive,
Hung men alive,
Compressing into one swift pang the slow
Three hours' agony, and looking down
With the beautiful, sad eyes of Christ beneath the
  thorny crown;
Brief on their lips a thwarted *"Sitio!"*
"I thirst!" . . . With Christ they cried,
Then—pinned to the planted wreckage—crucified
With Christ, they died.

Now for our comfort from the Holy Ghost
Come peace and sweetness and a holy pain—

[61]

And on Alaska's altar without stain
A sound that seems the breaking of the Host.

Laurel and tears for all
Who plunge unseen as wasted snowflakes fall
Dissolving in gray foam of wintry seas.
Tears and laurel and love
For these
Whom death found poised between two purities:
Whiteness below,
The unshadowed whiteness of Alaskan snow;
The white wings of the Holy Ghost above.

On the Drowning of Two Pupils

Beauty in books to boys who lean
   Idling on the sill of Spring,
Beauty to lads of seventeen
   In psalm and song I tried to bring.

But if one hoped to draw—I found—
   The tear of beauty to the eye,
Innocent Hylas must be drowned
   And every Juliet must die.

I might despair of ever joy
   Being attuned to Beauty's speech,
Did Death not sometimes take a boy
   And tutor strains I could not teach.

Loss of Faith

The life of grace and glory is the same.
The life of grace is, by another name,
Heaven on earth, and death is but a change
In range—
And nothing strange!

There is between our dreaming and our seeing
One pulsing continuity of being.
Ah, when the life of glory we achieve
Why grieve?
We only lose our having to believe!

Inspiration

We are so scarred with words and so bemused
By epithets incontinently fused,
That poets are but cripples till they find
And bathe in some Bethsaida of the mind.
We are so blind
To all the realm of real, so numb to feeling
Anything but the ache inside the breast,
It takes a miracle to make the healing
Miracle of beauty manifest.
"Will no man aid me to the waters?" None,
Though you lie moaning eight and thirty years.
Nor, languid like Narcissus in the sun,
Will you be cured because your face appears
When the surface clears.
"Will no man aid me?" Run,
Writhe, crawl, be somehow first—the hesitant
Will still be on the brink when wings are heard
And the waters by an angel visitant
To momentary potency are stirred!

PRINTED IN THE UNITED STATES OF AMERICA
BY J. J. LITTLE & IVES CO., NEW YORK